Fixing Toxic Workplaces

Leadership Strategies to Build a Positive Company Culture and Engage Employees

James Royce Smartman

Copyright © 2024 James Royce Smartman

All rights reserved.

DEDICATION

To the tenacious leaders and committed groups that work tirelessly every day to create inclusive, innovative, and trusting cultures. This book is for people who think that strong values and empowered individuals are the cornerstones of a successful corporation.

And to all the workers whose opinions have never been heard, may this work spur the change you are due.

CONTENTS

ACKNOWLEDGMENTS..1

CHAPTER 1..1

When Supervisors Don't Live Up to the Ideals..........................1

   1.1 Leadership Example Power...1

   1.2 Inconsistent Leadership's Ripple Effect..............................3

   1.3 Using Value-Driven Leadership to Restore Trust...............5

CHAPTER 2..9

It's Not Purposeful..9

   2.1 Outlining a Goal Apart from the Slogan.............................9

   2.2 Making Decisions Based on Purposes...............................11

   2.3 Matching Purpose to Teams..14

CHAPTER 3..18

Ignoring Feedback..18

   3.1 The Value of Hearing Employee Opinions........................18

   3.2 Systems of Effective Feedback...20

   3.3 Establishing a Culture of Feedback....................................23

CHAPTER 4..27

Bad Conduct Is Accepted..27

   4.1 Ignoring Toxic Behavior Has Costs....................................27

   4.2 Dealing Proactively with Negative Behavior....................29

   4.3 Clearly Defined Conduct Expectations..............................32

CHAPTER 5..37

Employing Based on Skills Rather Than Values............................ 37

    5.1 The Effects of Value Misalignment Over Time........................... 37

    5.2 Giving Cultural Fit Top Priority When Hiring............................ 39

    5.3 Cultural Integration Onboarding...43

CHAPTER 6...48

Cutting Culture...48

    6.1 Thinking Short-Term and Considering Long-Term Effects........... 48

    6.2 Culture's Contribution to Business Success.................................51

    6.3 Maintaining Culture in Difficult Times.. 54

CHAPTER 7...59

Social Engagement Is Not Encouraged..59

    7.1 The Value of Social Connections at Work..................................... 59

    7.2 Promoting Social Engagement to Increase Productivity................ 61

    7.3 Establishing a Connective Culture...64

CHAPTER 8...69

Using Pizza to Fill in the Gaps...69

    8.1 Cultural Issues Are Not Solved by Surface-Level Solutions.......... 69

    8.2 Sincere Attempts to Enhance Culture.. 71

    8.3 Appreciation of Employees Beyond Tangible Benefits.................. 74

CHAPTER 9...79

Cultural Imposition vs. Cultural Development....................................79

    9.1 Culture is Not Forced; It Is Organic... 79

    9.2 The Function of Leadership in Fostering Culture..........................81

    9.3 Fostering a Culture of Collaboration... 83

CHAPTER 10...88

For the sake of surveys..88

    10.1 Survey Fatigue: An Issue..88

    10.2 Using Input to Take Action..90

    10.3 Assessing Development After the Survey................... 92

ABOUT THE AUTHOR...96

ACKNOWLEDGMENTS

I want to express my sincere appreciation to everyone who helped to make this book possible. Above all, I want to express my sincere gratitude to my family and friends, whose constant encouragement and support have been my beacon of hope along this journey.

I am especially appreciative of my mentors and coworkers who so kindly shared their knowledge, experiences, and helpful criticism. Your insight has significantly enhanced the book's substance and influenced how I perceive organizational culture.

We would like to express our gratitude to the several experts and thought leaders in the fields of management and organizational development for their priceless research and contributions that made this examination of workplace culture possible.

I also want to thank the many leaders and staff members who told me their stories. Your experiences have motivated me to write this book and have highlighted the vital significance of creating a healthy work environment.

Finally, I would want to express my gratitude to my readers. It is because of your dedication to comprehending and enhancing company culture that this book exists. In your efforts to establish prosperous, welcoming, and active workplaces, I hope it proves to be a useful tool.

CHAPTER 1

WHEN SUPERVISORS DON'T LIVE UP TO THE IDEALS

1.1 Leadership Example Power

Any organization's culture is built on its leadership, and managers' actions are a clear indication of the company's basic principles. Managers that live according to these ideals set an example for their staff, directing them toward similar behaviors and mindsets. On the other hand, managers damage the organizational culture itself when they don't set a good example.

The impact of a leadership example goes well beyond what is expressly mentioned in business values or policies. Workers frequently imitate the actions of their leaders after observing them. When a manager exhibits honesty, teamwork, and creativity, staff members are more likely to absorb these qualities. On the other hand, managers convey a contradictory message when they fail to live up to the organization's values. Employee disenchantment results from the leadership's values becoming empty rhetoric.

- **The absence of integrity:** There is a perception of hypocrisy when managers talk about ethical behavior but behave unethically, such as by taking shortcuts or ignoring moral dilemmas.

- A culture of accountability is undermined by managers who don't hold themselves to the same standards as their team members.

- **Inconsistent Decision-Making**: Leaders who make choices that go against the company's declared values cause misunderstandings and make staff wonder if the company's values are really important.

It is impossible to overestimate the impact of setting a good example. When a management fails to uphold the values, it creates a precedent that allows staff members to ignore them as well.

1.2 Inconsistent Leadership's Ripple Effect

Every level of the organization may be severely impacted when the leadership does not share the company's values. Workers follow their leaders' lead, and when they see inconsistencies, it leads to disengagement, skepticism, and eventually a poisonous workplace.

There are various ways that the ripple effect might appear:

The act of disengagement When workers perceive a discrepancy between their bosses' actions and the company's declared values, they get demotivated. They begin to doubt the sincerity of the organization's goal, which may lead to less effort and production.

- **Erosion of Trust:** In any company, trust is essential. Trust erodes when workers believe their leaders are not upholding the principles. This impairs teamwork and collaboration in addition to having an impact on daily operations.

- **Apathy Culture:** Employees may develop an indifferent mindset if supervisors fail to provide an example of virtues like creativity or accountability. The general attitude shifts to "If the boss doesn't care, why should I?" which lowers the caliber of the job produced generally.

- **The promotion of toxic behavior:** Toxic behaviors among employees can grow if supervisors condone or even participate in actions that go against the company's ideals. For instance, if a manager condones dishonesty or bullying, staff members might feel free to act in the same way since they think there won't be any actual repercussions.

Inconsistent leadership has the long-term potential to turn a once-vibrant and cohesive organization into a dysfunctional setting where turnover, discontent, and misunderstandings are common. The ripple effect will keep growing in the absence of strong, values-driven leadership, making it more difficult to keep people in line with the company's goals.

1.3 Using Value-Driven Leadership to Restore Trust

A purposeful, values-based strategy is needed to repair a culture that has been harmed by inconsistency in leadership. Rebuilding trust within the organization and between managers and their staff is the first step in this process. The ideals that managers want others to uphold must be exemplified by them. Value-driven leadership is actively embodying values in all choices, deeds, and relationships rather than merely articulating them.

The following are crucial actions to restore confidence and realign leadership with business values:

Development and Training: Continuous training and development is one of the best strategies to make sure managers live up to the company's values. Managers can be given the tools they need to lead by example through leadership programs that emphasize ethics, emotional intelligence, and value-based decision-making.

- Encourage managers to take part in ethical

leadership seminars or workshops.

- Enable aspiring managers to observe established leaders modeling value-driven leadership through mentorship programs.

Reliable Assessment: In addition to performance measures, managers should be assessed on how well they support and uphold the company's values. By including values in performance evaluations, leaders are held responsible for upholding the culture.

- Establish 360-degree feedback systems that allow peers, subordinates, and superiors to evaluate how well managers exhibit the values.

- Establish quantifiable, explicit objectives for value-based leadership as part of yearly performance reviews.

Open and honest communication: Leadership must communicate openly in order to restore trust. Managers should clearly lay out a plan for realignment and publicly admit any prior shortcomings in upholding the standards. Managers can start to rebuild their reputation by admitting their errors and making a commitment to improve.

- Organize town hall gatherings when managers speak to the entire staff about value-driven leadership.

- Promote frank discussions in which staff members feel comfortable offering input on leadership practices that either support or contradict the principles.

Setting a Good Example: Consistency is the most important component of value-driven leadership. Values must be displayed by managers not just when it's opportune but also during difficult times. Workers closely observe how leaders respond to conflicts, crises, and high-stress circumstances. Managers must set an example of moral conduct, equity, and responsibility at these times.

- Managers should be encouraged to lead with humility and accept responsibility for their errors.

- Emphasize the value of equity in all decision-making, especially when it comes to areas like awards, promotions, and disciplinary measures.

Rebuilding trust requires constant dedication to value-driven leadership rather than a one-time endeavor. Managers provide a powerful, unambiguous example for the entire staff when they continuously live up to the values. In the long run, this not only mends the harm caused by past leadership blunders but also fortifies the culture as a whole, increasing employee loyalty, engagement, and long-term success.

There are serious repercussions when managers don't live up to the organization's ideals. It erodes culture, engagement, and trust. However, firms may not only recover but also cultivate a stronger, more aligned workplace where leaders and people are united in purpose and action by committing to value-driven leadership. The company's ideals are held together by its leadership, and when it is strong, the entire organization prospers.

CHAPTER 2

It's Not Purposeful

2.1 Outlining a Goal Apart from the Slogan

The idea of corporate purpose in today's business environment has developed much beyond memorable catch phrases or marketing taglines. The core of a company's identity is its purpose, which outlines the organization's goals and the reasons behind its existence. However, for many firms, purpose is still a high concept that isn't tied to the day-to-day operations, which creates a gulf between employees and leadership. Employees may believe that their contributions don't fit with the larger company goal or that their job is meaningless as a result of this disconnect, which can be detrimental.

A purpose is just meaningless language if it is not carried out and incorporated into the workplace culture. Employees need to understand how their specific roles relate to the overall goal for it to have a real impact. This is more than just learning a mission statement by heart. Workers must comprehend how their everyday tasks advance the objectives of the business and ultimately affect the community, society, or clients.

Closing the Gap Between positions and Purpose: Businesses need to create an atmosphere where the organization's purpose is well-defined, expressed, and connected to certain positions. Workers should believe that their efforts are contributing to the company's mission and that they are a part of something bigger. This link can be established by:

1. **Regular Communication:** Through meetings, newsletters, and other internal communications, leadership should consistently reaffirm the goal.
2. **Job Role Clarification:** Managers and supervisors need to assist staff members in comprehending how their work fits into the overall scheme of things.
3. **Performance Reviews:** Purpose should be linked to performance reviews, wherein workers are rewarded for their efforts that support and advance the organization's goal.

Steer clear of the generic purpose statement trap: Many businesses make the mistake of crafting generic or ambiguous purpose statements that don't connect with their workforce. Purpose needs to be clear, action-oriented, and accessible in order to genuinely inspire and engage. The company's beliefs, objectives for the future, and distinctive position within its industry should all be reflected in its purpose.

The goal of defining purpose beyond the slogan is to integrate it into the organization's core values. A more engaged, motivated, and cohesive workplace can result from employees who not only understand but also feel a sense of belonging to the company's mission.

2.2 Making Decisions Based on Purposes

At every level of the business, choices must be made with purpose in mind, not only as a guiding concept. making decisions with a purpose is essential to make sure that the business's activities continuously support its mission and give stakeholders and workers a sense of legitimacy and trust. But far too frequently, choices are chosen more for convenience or short-term financial objectives than for the company's main objective, which causes dissonance that staff members can readily detect.

Before making strategic decisions, senior leadership must constantly question, "Does this align with our purpose?" in order to practice purpose-driven decision-making. This includes choices pertaining to:

1. **Product Development:** Are the goods and services we provide in line with our mission, or are they only made to make as much money as possible? For instance, a company's product line should include eco-friendly options if its goal is to increase environmental sustainability.
2. **Hiring and Talent Management:** Are we employing individuals who are as dedicated to the company's mission as we are? Purpose-driven businesses frequently place more importance on shared values and cultural fit than merely technical credentials. Workers are more likely to be involved and motivated if they share the company's vision.

3. **Communication and Customer Engagement:** How do we explain our mission to our clients? Through ethical business methods, transparent marketing, or customer service, purpose-driven organizations make sure that every connection with their clientele represents their underlying values.

4. **Corporate Social Responsibility (CSR):** Are we fulfilling our mission beyond generating profits? In order to further show their dedication to societal or environmental goals, many businesses incorporate their purpose into their CSR operations by funding causes that align with their mission.

Not only can purpose-driven decision-making help executives, but it also gives workers a sense of empowerment by connecting their job to a greater purpose. More buy-in and engagement are the results of employees feeling that their efforts are valued when they witness their leaders making choices that align with the company's mission.

Additionally, making decisions with a purpose promotes long-term success. Businesses that put their goal ahead of short-term profits typically have better relationships with both staff and clients, which boosts consumer loyalty and trust and gives them a competitive advantage in the market.

2.3 Matching Purpose to Teams

The next crucial step in making sure that the company's mission is ingrained at every level of the business is to align teams with purpose. Teams will get disoriented and disengaged if a mission isn't consistently conveyed, discussed, and reviewed. Teams are more likely to be cohesive, driven, and effective when they comprehend and support the organization's mission.

The following tactics can assist in bringing teams into line with the mission of the business:

Frequent Reaffirmation of Goals: Team meetings, planning sessions, and employee interactions should all regularly revisit the company's mission. Leaders should remind staff members of the "why" behind their job, especially when launching new projects or during difficult circumstances. This fosters a robust and steady culture of purpose.

- **Town Hall Gatherings:** Call frequent meetings to provide staff members an update on how the organization is fulfilling its mission and how various teams are helping to achieve it.
- **Intentional Workshops:** Plan training sessions that emphasize how staff members at all levels may incorporate the company's mission into their everyday responsibilities and decision-making procedures.

Setting Purpose-Driven Goals: Connecting the company's mission to quantifiable objectives is necessary to align teams with purpose. The company's ultimate mission must be reflected and supported when establishing goals, whether they be departmental, organizational, or personal. For instance, research and development, innovative problem-solving, and cooperative ventures that push boundaries should be given top priority if a company's mission is to foster innovation.

- **Team-Level Objectives:** To ensure that staff members comprehend how their work fits into the larger mission, managers should assist their teams in establishing goals that are directly related to the company's purpose.

- **Individual Accountability:** During performance reviews or goal-setting activities, encourage staff members to explain how their individual efforts contribute to the company's mission.

Fostering Purpose Through Recognition: One of the best ways to encourage involvement and reaffirm the significance of the mission is to acknowledge and celebrate contributions that meet the company's purpose. Recognizing employees for living up to the company's mission sets an example that others will want to follow.

- **Purpose-Driven Awards:** Put in place recognition initiatives that honor staff members who exhibit behavior consistent with the mission of the business.
- **Team Celebrations:** To motivate others, highlight certain initiatives or group efforts that have advanced the company's goals and publicly acknowledge these successes.

Use as a Filter for Decisions: When making decisions, teams should be encouraged to apply the company's mission as a filter. Every debate should start with the question, "Does this align with our purpose?" while determining which projects to prioritize, what tactics to pursue, or how to distribute resources. By doing this, teams maintain their attention on the important things and keep in line with the long-term goals of the business rather than focusing on temporary diversions.

Purpose must be lived, integrated, and actively pursued; it is not merely a statement that appears on a business's website or an inspirational poster at the workplace. Establishing a strong link between the company's mission and the daily responsibilities of its employees is necessary to define purpose beyond the tagline. An organization's feeling of meaning and trust are increased when purpose is continuously incorporated into decision-making.

Teams need to be consistently in line with the organization's mission to succeed and stay motivated, making sure that each task, choice, and objective advances the overarching objective. Employees at a purpose-driven company are not just inspired; they are also propelled toward sustained engagement and achievement.

CHAPTER 3

IGNORING FEEDBACK

3.1 The Value of Hearing Employee Opinions

Feedback is an essential instrument for development, growth, and ongoing improvement in any kind of company. Employees can express problems, suggestions, and chances for change, and it offers insights that leadership might not be able to perceive from their perspective. However, employees receive a clear message that their opinions are unimportant when feedback is routinely disregarded. This eventually results in a poisonous work climate where people feel underappreciated and disengaged, as well as despair and frustration.

- **The effect on morale:** Workers are more prone to lose interest in their jobs if they believe their opinions are not valued. They gradually give up trying, stop caring, and stop participating. This disengagement may show itself as increased turnover rates, diminished teamwork, and decreased output.

- **Lost Possibilities for Enhancement:** Feedback frequently includes insightful details about inefficiencies, ways to improve customer service, and innovations that could help the business. Ignoring input is a lost chance to improve the organization's operations as a whole as well as to resolve employee problems. Since they are on the front lines, employees' opinions are crucial in helping to create improved procedures and policies.

- **Reduction in Communication and Trust:** When staff members offer input, they put their faith in the leadership's ability to act on it. Neglecting input on a regular basis damages the connection between management and staff by undermining trust. Employees grow reluctant to voice their opinions over time, and this communication failure can lead to a culture of silence where issues continue to fester unchecked.

It's not only about getting input from employees; it's also about showing that management appreciates and values their efforts. Any healthy organization's basis may start to deteriorate in the absence of this.

3.2 Systems of Effective Feedback

Feedback needs to be captured, analyzed, and acted upon by structured processes in order to have an impact. Because they lack the tools to handle it efficiently or because the leadership doesn't value it, many firms don't take employee input seriously. A strong, reliable, and open feedback system will guarantee that workers' opinions are heard and their suggestions are treated seriously.

- **Unidentified Surveys:** Anonymous surveys are among the best methods for getting candid employee input. Employees are encouraged to express their opinions anonymously without worrying about bias or retaliation. These questionnaires must be designed to collect both qualitative information (such as open-ended questions for workplace enhancements) and quantitative data (such as satisfaction ratings). Surveys conducted on a regular basis, whether quarterly or biannually, enable businesses to monitor trends over time and evaluate the success of any adjustments made.

- **One-on-One Consultations:** Even though anonymous surveys are great for getting feedback from a large number of people, they should be used in conjunction with more direct, intimate communication methods like one-on-one meetings. Team members' experiences, difficulties, and recommendations for development should be discussed at regular meetings between managers and team members. This makes it a two-way channel of communication and gives workers a chance to get feedback on how they're doing.

- **Digital platforms and suggestion boxes:** Companies can offer open avenues for input, such as digital and physical suggestion boxes or specialized web platforms, in addition to formal meetings or surveys. By making it simple for staff members to voice their thoughts or complaints at any time, these platforms should promote an environment where employees view feedback as an ongoing and essential aspect of company operations.

- **Accountability and Follow-Up:** After the data is gathered, the feedback process continues. Businesses need to examine the comments, spot trends, and make adjustments as needed. Additionally, it's critical to follow up with employees to let them know that their opinions are valued. Transparency and accountability are ensured by disclosing survey or discussion results and action plans for resolving issues.

- **Loops of Feedback for Ongoing Improvement:** Good feedback systems should function as loops in which staff are continually updated on progress and feedback is routinely requested, assessed, and implemented. Organizations show that they respect input and use it to make real improvements by closing the feedback loop.

Effectively putting these mechanisms in place promotes candid communication and guarantees that comments are used to spur constructive change rather than being ignored in reports.

3.3 Establishing a Culture of Feedback

Feedback needs to be ingrained in the organization's culture in order to genuinely spur innovation and advancement. A feedback culture is one in which staff members are at ease expressing their opinions because they know that doing so will result in significant action. Additionally, it's a culture that encourages open communication between coworkers, between staff and management, and between leadership and staff.

1. **Promoting Open Communication:** A culture that values and encourages feedback must be actively promoted by leadership. This calls for fostering psychological safety; workers must be assured that voicing their candid thoughts, even if they are critical, won't have unfavorable repercussions. Instead of waiting for feedback to be provided,

leaders should routinely solicit it. Asking open-ended inquiries like "How can I support your work?" or "What can we do better?" encourages feedback in a non-threatening manner.

- **Acknowledging and rewarding constructive criticism:** Making sure staff members understand the significance of their efforts is a component of developing a feedback culture. Leadership should acknowledge the staff members or groups involved when feedback results in a change, demonstrating that their opinions mattered. The message that input is valued is reinforced when contributions are acknowledged, whether through internal newsletters, meetings, or rewards.

- **Constructive Feedback Training:** It typically takes training, especially in the area of constructive criticism and feedback-giving, to establish a feedback culture. Managers ought to receive professional training on how to respond to criticism so that it is not interpreted as a personal jab but rather as a chance for development. In a similar vein, staff members ought to receive training on how to give detailed, useful, and solution-focused feedback.

Starting at the top:

- **Modeling:** A feedback culture is shaped by its leaders. Senior leaders will influence the rest of the organization if they are receptive to criticism and demonstrate a readiness to make changes in response to suggestions from others. In order to set an example for their teams, leaders should aggressively seek out input from them and respond to it with humility and attentiveness.

- **Feedback as an Innovation Driver:** Businesses with a culture that values feedback are typically more creative and flexible. Feedback can help discover new problems, inspire innovative solutions, and keep the business flexible in a market that is constantly evolving. Businesses can access a common reservoir of ideas that inspire new breakthroughs by consistently listening to their staff.

One of the quickest ways to undermine participation, undermine trust, and limit creativity in a company is to ignore input. Missed chances for advancement mount over time, and workers who don't feel heard soon lose desire. Companies must create strong feedback mechanisms and foster a feedback-driven culture where employee opinions are respected and taken into consideration in order to avoid this.

Organizations can guarantee that workers stay engaged, issues are resolved before they worsen, and innovative ideas keep the business moving forward by giving priority to feedback, developing efficient mechanisms to collect it, and cultivating a culture where it is valued and rewarded.

CHAPTER 4

BAD CONDUCT IS ACCEPTED

4.1 Ignoring Toxic Behavior Has Costs

The repercussions of allowing bad behavior in the workplace go much beyond the acts of one person. Employee morale and productivity are severely harmed by toxic personnel, who act disrespectfully, hostilely, or in other disruptive ways. Unchecked behavior has a cascading impact that erodes trust, weakens team cohesiveness, and may result in the departure of talented workers.

- **Deterioration of Team Spirit:** It is easy to spread toxic conduct. Others may become disillusioned if one employee continuously behaves badly with no repercussions. When high-achieving, courteous team members see that their efforts to sustain a positive work environment are not appreciated, they are more prone to disengage or lose motivation. Resentment, annoyance, and a general drop in morale result from this.

- **Raise in Turnover:** Stress, anxiety, and job discontent are frequently elevated in workers exposed to toxic behavior. This eventually results in burnout and a higher chance of turnover. Particularly high-performing workers are more likely to quit a company that ignores toxicity. Replacing skilled employees comes at a high cost, not just in monetary terms but also in the form of lost institutional knowledge, interrupted projects, and decreased team productivity.

- **Damage to Innovation and Team Collaboration:** In addition to upsetting interpersonal relationships, toxic employees inhibit creativity and teamwork. Employees are less inclined to take chances, offer ideas, or solve problems creatively when they feel intimidated, insulted, or ignored. Because toxicity creates a culture of fear, workers put their own survival ahead of the success of the team. As a result, the company is unable to innovate and leverage its most important asset, the collective intelligence of its employees.

- **Damage to Reputation:** In the connected world of today, an organization's internal culture frequently gets known to the outside world. A company's reputation may suffer if it is recognized for putting up with bad behavior. This can have an influence on relationships with clients, partners, and other stakeholders in addition to talent recruitment, since prospective employees will steer clear of toxic workplaces.

In the end, there are significant hidden and obvious consequences associated with disregarding bad behavior. These expenses have an impact on the business's long-term success, bottom line, and capacity to draw in and keep top individuals.

4.2 Dealing Proactively with Negative Behavior

It is a failure of leadership to tolerate bad behavior. In order to make it apparent that toxic behavior will not be accepted, managers must deal with negative behavior in a timely and proactive manner. Employees feel protected, appreciated, and empowered to perform at their highest level when problems are addressed head-on.

- **The manager's responsibility is as follows:** Supervisors need to have the abilities and self-assurance to deal with bad behavior. This entails giving candid, helpful criticism and engaging in challenging dialogue with staff members who display unfavorable habits. Whether it's rudeness, bullying, or unprofessional behavior, a successful leader confronts problems head-on with the intention of fostering a supportive, productive workplace.

- **The Function of Training:** Training is frequently necessary for proactive management of undesirable conduct. In addition to conflict resolution training, managers must learn how to spot toxic conduct early on before it gets out of hand. Modules on how to effectively enforce behavioral norms, handle challenging conversations, and offer constructive criticism should be a regular part of leadership development programs.

- **Quick and Forceful Action:** It's critical to act swiftly and forcefully when bad behavior is noticed. Negative behavior should never be ignored since doing so conveys the incorrect message that the leadership is unconcerned or that the behavior is acceptable. Dealing with toxic personnel as soon as possible helps stop their behavior from having a detrimental impact on the team as a whole. Furthermore, prompt action establishes a standard for others and shows that the company is committed to preserving its ideals and fostering a positive workplace culture.

- **Offering Assistance and Remedies:** Punitive punishment is not always necessary to address bad behavior. Employees frequently might not realize the consequences of their conduct, or they may be dealing with personal issues that influence their behavior. In order to help the employee get well, managers should handle these circumstances with compassion and provide resources, coaching, or therapy. Correcting the behavior while preserving a sense of support and accountability is the aim.

Managers reaffirm the company's dedication to creating a courteous and upbeat work environment by taking proactive measures to remediate unfavorable conduct. In addition to preserving team spirit, this fosters an accountable culture where all workers are held to high standards.

4.3 Clearly Defined Conduct Expectations

A positive workplace culture is built on clear behavioral rules. Employees might not fully comprehend what constitutes appropriate behavior in the absence of clear rules, which could result in inconsistent handling of various situations. A clear code of conduct establishes the tone for a polite, welcoming workplace and guarantees that everyone is in agreement with the organization's ideals and expectations.

The significance of adhering to a code of conduct A code of conduct clarifies the kinds of behavior that will not be accepted in the workplace and describes the behaviors that are required. This paper ought to be thorough, addressing topics like cooperation, communication, inclusion, respect, and conflict resolution. A robust code of conduct guarantees that everyone is aware of what is expected of them and serves as a point of reference for both management and staff.

- **Regular Enforcement:** The effectiveness of behavioral rules is contingent upon their consistent enforcement. Regardless of an employee's position or standing within the organization, leadership must be dedicated to enforcing the code of conduct at all times. Perceptions of unfairness or partiality brought on by inconsistent enforcement can erode confidence in the leadership. All workers should be held to the same standards, regardless of their position—from senior executives to junior team members.

- **Frequent Training and Communication:** Standards for behavior shouldn't be constant. Through continual training and development initiatives, organizations must routinely convey their expectations to their workforce. Workshops covering subjects like communication, workplace respect, and diversity and inclusion can aid in reiterating the significance of the code of conduct. To make sure the standards are still applicable and represent the changing culture of the company, it's also critical to review them from time to time.

- **Establishing a Reporting System:** Workers must be able to report infractions of the code of conduct in a secure and private manner. Poor behavior may go undetected in the absence of an efficient reporting system because people may be skeptical that action would be taken or fear reprisals. Businesses should set up several channels for people to report issues, including internet platforms, anonymous hotlines, and human resources. Additionally, it's critical that reports undergo a comprehensive and unbiased investigation and that, when required, the proper action be taken.

- **Encouraging Positive Conduct:** Setting explicit behavioral guidelines serves the dual purposes of rewarding and promoting good behavior in addition to discouraging bad behavior. Employees that continuously exhibit the virtues of integrity, respect, and teamwork should be honored by the leadership. Peer nominations, official recognition programs, or even unofficial acclaim can accomplish this. By rewarding good behavior, you can encourage others to adopt the desired culture.

Tolerating bad behavior at work is an expensive error that impacts the organization's long-term success in addition to employee morale and productivity. One of the most important leadership responsibilities is to deal with toxic conduct in a timely and proactive manner. Organizations can cultivate a work environment that values accountability, respect, and teamwork by enforcing regulations consistently, establishing clear behavioral standards, and developing a feedback culture.

A clear code of conduct and proactive handling of unfavorable behavior guarantee that all staff members share the company's values and are aware of the repercussions of breaking them. By doing this, businesses can preserve their culture, keep their best employees, and lay a solid basis for long-term success.

CHAPTER 5

Employing Based on Skills Rather Than Values

5.1 The Effects of Value Misalignment Over Time

Although technical proficiency is necessary for work performance, hiring someone purely on the basis of talent without taking values into account might have negative long-term impacts on a company's culture. There is a rift between the team and the individual when a corporation hires people whose personal beliefs diverge from the organization's basic values. This imbalance has the potential to weaken trust, decrease teamwork, and create a poisonous atmosphere over time.

- **Fragmented Team Dynamics:** Team cohesiveness can be harmed by workers who are technically skilled but do not share the organization's ideals. For instance, conflict arises when a business encourages teamwork yet employs a person who prefers to work alone and doesn't participate in group initiatives. Members of the team may feel excluded or underappreciated, which lowers morale and decreases output.

- **Corporate Culture Erosion:** Hiring individuals who don't share the company's ideals can eventually weaken its culture. When workers with different objectives or attitudes affect the workplace, the common sense of purpose and dedication to principles starts to wane. This might cause misunderstandings regarding the company's values and make it challenging for the leadership to preserve a solid, cohesive culture.

- A higher rate of employee turnover Because their behavior is inconsistent with the organization's expectations or because they feel out of place, employees who don't share the company's values are more likely to quit. In addition to the costs associated with hiring and training new employees, high turnover rates often generate team instability and disruption. Employee morale may also be further impacted when they witness coworkers departing because of cultural misalignment, which can cause fear and uncertainty.

- **Damage to Reputation:** Employers may find it difficult to draw in top talent if their hiring procedures are inconsistent or out of alignment. If an organization is seen as prioritizing talents over the moral, cultural, or social elements that characterize it, word will get out fast. Prospective workers are increasingly drawn to organizations that integrate values such as social responsibility, diversity, and honesty into day-to-day operations.

Long-term success is ultimately at risk when recruiting is done solely on the basis of talents and not beliefs. Businesses need to understand that maintaining organizational health requires cultural fit, which is not merely a nice-to-have.

5.2 Giving Cultural Fit Top Priority When Hiring

Employers who hire for cultural fit are guaranteed to share

the organization's values and vision in addition to having the necessary technical skills. A more harmonious, involved, and effective staff is the result of this alignment.

- **Establishing Fundamental Principles in the Hiring Process:** Organizations must have a clear knowledge of their basic principles and how they should be reflected in day-to-day operations before concentrating on cultural fit. What does actual teamwork look like? In what ways is respect shown at work? How is decision-making influenced by innovation? Following their precise definition, these need to be included into all aspects of the hiring process, including interview questions and job descriptions.

- **Value assessments and behavioral interviews:** Beyond asking technical questions, a well-structured interview process should also look for cultural fit. Employing behavioral interviewing techniques, which ask candidates to give instances of how they have handled particular situations in the past, is a good way to assess how well they connect with the company's values. Asking a candidate how they contributed to a successful team project, for example, can reveal information about their collaborative approach if cooperation is a key value.

- **Emotional Intelligence and Soft Skills Assessment:** The ability of an employee to manage complicated social dynamics, communicate effectively, and empathize with coworkers is typically the deciding factor in cultural fit. These "soft skills" can occasionally be more crucial to an organization's long-term success than hard skills. Relationship management, conflict resolution, and cultural adaptation all depend heavily on emotional intelligence. During the hiring process, instruments like role-playing games or personality tests can be used to assess a candidate's soft skills.

- **Participating in the Hiring Process with Team Members:** Incorporating prospective co workers into the hiring process guarantees that the applicant gets assessed from a variety of angles, especially about their likelihood of collaborating with the team.

Current staff can determine whether a candidate shares their beliefs and working style through team-based interviews or group discussions, fostering an inclusive and cohesive decision-making process.

- **Skills and Fit in Balance:** Prioritizing cultural fit is important, but talents should never be sacrificed for this. A candidate who succeeds in both areas is desirable. However, teaching someone technical skills is frequently simpler than changing their conduct or ideals. Therefore, firms should think about the long-term benefits of emphasizing values when choosing between a highly talented recruit who doesn't connect with company values and a moderately skilled candidate who is a fantastic cultural fit.

Employers may create teams that are not just capable but also unified in their dedication to common objectives and values by making sure that cultural fit is a top consideration when making hiring decisions.

5.3 Cultural Integration Onboarding

Onboarding is a crucial chance to integrate new workers into the company's culture and reaffirm the ideals they were hired to uphold, not just to help them get used to their job duties. The goal of the onboarding process should be to make new hires feel supported, accepted, and in line with the organization's vision right away.

- **Prioritizing cultural orientation:** The company's history, mission, vision, and values should all be covered in a thorough onboarding program. This aids new hires in comprehending the organization's overarching goal and their place within it. Cultural orientation should incorporate expectations for behavior, communication, teamwork, and decision-making in addition to technical instruction. Many prosperous businesses take advantage of this opportunity to tell tales and provide examples of how their principles have influenced significant business choices and turning points.

- Peer support and mentorship: During the onboarding process, matching new hires with a buddy or mentor can significantly improve cultural assimilation. Mentors serve as role models for how the company's principles are applied in day-to-day interactions in addition to offering advice on the technical aspects of the work. Peer support gives new hires a sense of community with their coworkers and a safe place to ask concerns about the job and workplace culture.

- **Value Reinforcement via Training and Development:** Specific training sessions that reaffirm the company's principles and describe how they are used in day-to-day operations should be part of the onboarding process. Employees should be introduced to the company's brainstorming, experimenting, and creative problem-solving procedures, for instance, if innovation is a key value. Training may stress the value of empathy and active listening in client interactions if customer focus is a top concern.

- The process of assimilating into the workplace culture doesn't stop after the initial weeks. Organizations should provide continual opportunities for cultural immersion if they want to genuinely integrate values. Regular team-building exercises, values-based leadership seminars, or quarterly performance assessments that assess both performance and alignment with the organization's values are a few examples of this. Through rewards, acknowledgment, and communication, leadership must continuously reaffirm cultural messages.

- **Promoting Bidirectional Feedback:** Feedback channels for new hires to discuss their experiences and recommend changes should be part of the onboarding process. This aids businesses in determining whether new hires are internalizing the company's values and how well the onboarding program is performing. Leaders ought to promote candid communication and make use of this input to keep improving the onboarding procedure.

Businesses may guarantee that new hires are not only

ready for their positions but also completely in line with the organization's values and expectations by emphasizing cultural integration during the onboarding process. Since engaged, motivated, and loyal employees are more likely to sense a connection to the company's objective, this early investment in cultural alignment lays the groundwork for long-term success.

If values are not taken into account while hiring, it can result in long-term issues that compromise a company's productivity and culture. Value misalignment causes strained relationships within the team, low morale, and more turnover. Organizations may make sure that new hires not only have the requisite abilities but also exemplify the values that are essential to the company's identity by giving cultural fit top priority during the hiring process.

Onboarding is a crucial phase in integrating new hires into the company culture once they are employed. A solid onboarding procedure lays the groundwork for sustained engagement, promotes peer support, and reaffirms the company's values. Employers who place a high priority on values and skills during the hiring and onboarding process build unified, productive teams that support the organization's mission and lead to long-term success.

CHAPTER 6

CUTTING CULTURE

6.1 Thinking Short-Term and Considering Long-Term Effects

Companies are frequently tempted to reduce investments in culture-related initiatives like team-building exercises, wellness benefits, and employee engagement programs during lean financial times. These programs are occasionally seen as unnecessary "extras" rather than essential elements of a successful company. This strategy, however, is indicative of short-term thinking and may have serious long-term repercussions.

- **Deterioration of Morale and Trust:** Employees frequently interpret a company's reduction in culture-building initiatives as an indication that management is putting cost reductions ahead of their welfare. These initiatives show a company's dedication to its employees and go beyond simple benefits. Leadership runs the risk of undermining staff confidence in the company by reducing these efforts. Workers may become disengaged, less motivated, and less productive if they believe that the organization does not respect their efforts or is not as invested in their long-term success.

- **Decreased Engagement of Employees:** The goal of employee engagement programs is to promote connection, creativity, and a feeling of community, whether they take the form of social gatherings, wellness initiatives, or professional development opportunities. Employee disengagement could result from the reduction or elimination of these initiatives, which would lower job satisfaction. Research continuously demonstrates that motivated workers are more inventive, dedicated, and productive. Companies are sacrificing the very things that motivate performance and retention by discontinuing these initiatives.

- **Impact on Collaboration and Innovation:**

Initiatives aimed at enhancing company culture frequently provide workers the room and chance to work together and come up with new ideas. Companies hinder the unofficial contacts and team dynamics that foster innovation when they prioritize short-term cost reductions by discontinuing these programs. Long-term, the organization becomes less flexible and agile as a result of the suppression of innovation caused by the absence of these interactions.

- **Raise in Turnover:** Workers are more likely to stick with organizations that show a sincere interest in their development and well-being. Employees, especially those who appreciate a positive, encouraging work atmosphere, may begin looking for possibilities elsewhere if cultural investments are reduced. The financial stability of the organization is further weakened by high turnover rates, which result in increased expenses for hiring, onboarding, and training.

Although reducing culture might seem like a simple

solution to short-term financial issues, the long-term harm it causes to employee engagement, morale, and retention can be far more expensive. Businesses that put short-term financial comfort ahead of long-term cultural sustainability run the danger of losing their competitive edge and failing in the long run.

6.2 Culture's Contribution to Business Success

One of the most important factors influencing success in contemporary firms is a robust corporate culture. Culture is a vital resource that influences employee behavior, spurs innovation, and increases employee loyalty. It goes beyond simply making the workplace comfortable. Reducing culture-building initiatives may provide financial relief in the short term, but it may have serious long-term repercussions.

- **Retention of Employees:** Strong organizational cultures result in lower employee turnover since staff members are better bonded to the company and its principles. Loyalty is fostered by a good corporate culture, and workers are more inclined to stick with a business where they feel appreciated and supported. Employees may feel disengaged from the organization's goals and objectives if culture is deprioritized, which increases the likelihood that they may depart for rival companies that provide a better working environment.

- **Improved Performance and Productivity:** Employee engagement increases productivity. Employees are motivated to give their best work when the corporate culture prioritizes cooperation, trust, and ongoing learning. Culture serves as a compass that influences how workers approach their jobs, communicate with coworkers, and resolve issues. Companies lose this driving power when they reduce their cultural initiatives, which eventually affects performance and the bottom line.

- **Creativity and Innovation:** Risk-taking, creative thinking, and cross-departmental collaboration are all encouraged by a vibrant culture. A positive company culture encourages open communication, cross-functional teamwork, and informal talks, all of which lead to creative solutions to business problems. Businesses run the danger of limiting innovation, which is crucial for expansion and preserving a competitive edge, if they lack a solid cultural foundation.

- **Reputation of the brand and customer satisfaction:** Because they feel empowered and inspired to represent the business in a positive way, employees who share the company's culture and values typically offer better customer service. Better client experiences result from a strong internal culture, which boosts the company's reputation and encourages repeat business. Reducing cultural investments can lead to disengaged workers who are less inclined to go above and beyond for clients, which can eventually harm the brand's reputation.

- **Bringing in Top Talent:** Companies with strong cultures attract top talent in today's fiercely competitive job market. Candidates want to work in settings that support their values, offer chances for advancement, and foster a feeling of purpose; they are not merely searching for a salary. Businesses that disregard their culture may find it difficult to draw in and keep top talent, especially as younger workers place a greater value on work-life balance and corporate culture.

Essentially, a company's culture is an investment in its future prosperity. It lays the groundwork for resiliency, creativity, and consistent performance—even in the face of adversity. Reducing culture-building initiatives may result in short-term financial gains, but the long-term costs of lost competitive advantage, higher turnover, and decreased productivity are far higher.

6.3 Maintaining Culture in Difficult Times

It takes innovative leadership and a strong dedication to the organization's principles to sustain a strong culture in the face of economic difficulties. Cutting culture could seem like the simplest way to deal with mounting financial strains, but leaders must figure out how to maintain and even enhance cultural identity in these trying times.

- **Reassessing Non-Financial Rewards:** Not every culture-building project necessitates a large financial outlay. Leaders should shift their attention to non-monetary incentives that still boost participation and morale, even though budget cuts could force them to cut back on some programs or benefits. Recognizing staff accomplishments, encouraging scheduling flexibility, and providing chances for professional growth through internal training or mentoring are a few examples. These programs can encourage dedication and a feeling of community without incurring large expenses.

- **Promoting Free and Open Communication:** Employees may worry about the company's future or their job security during trying times. Leadership must communicate openly and honestly in order to preserve engagement and confidence. Employees can feel more confident that their leaders are dedicated to the long-term success of the company if they receive regular briefings on its financial status, strategic choices, and future plans. A more resilient, cohesive workforce is produced by leaders that pay attention to their staff members' worries and include them in problem-solving.

- **Giving Core Cultural Elements Priority:** While not all cultural projects must be preserved in their original form, the company's values, mission, and dedication to its employees should all be preserved. The elements of culture that are most directly related to the identity and success of the company should be preserved by leaders. This could entail cutting down on some initiatives while stepping up others that are more crucial to preserving a welcoming, inclusive workplace.

- **Encouraging Managers to Maintain Culture:** In times of adversity, managers are essential to preserving culture. Even in situations where resources are scarce, leadership should give managers the instruments and direction they require to create a productive workplace. This could entail teaching managers how to lead with empathy, provide emotional support to their people, and uphold the company's values in their daily interactions. Managers may assist keep team morale high and reduce disengagement by setting an example of positive behavior and upholding cultural norms.

- **Promoting Networks of Peer Support:** Giving workers the chance to help one another helps improve culture, particularly during difficult times. Social networks within the organization, cross-functional cooperation, and peer mentorship programs can all help people feel like they belong. Employees are more likely to remain involved and dedicated to the company's objectives, especially during trying times, when they have a support network and a sense of belonging to their coworkers.

A crucial leadership difficulty that can be overcome with careful, innovative techniques is maintaining culture during uncertain or economic times. Organizations that are able to preserve their strong cultural identity in the face of cost-cutting or initiative reductions are the ones that survive challenging times. Businesses can continue to prosper while maintaining the characteristics that make them special and prosperous by emphasizing communication, encouraging a feeling of community, and utilizing non-monetary incentives.

Saving money by reducing culture is a temporary solution that can have disastrous long-term effects. Even though it might offer short-term financial respite, businesses will ultimately pay more in lost productivity, increased employee attrition, and damaged brand reputation as a result of the loss of engagement, innovation, and trust. Culture is a key component of an organization's success and cannot be replaced.

Maintaining the essential components of corporate culture, coming up with innovative ways to engage staff, and upholding the company's ideals without depending entirely on financial investment must be the top priorities for executives during difficult times. By doing this, they may maintain employee morale, encourage loyalty, and set up the business for long-term success.

CHAPTER 7

SOCIAL ENGAGEMENT IS NOT ENCOURAGED

7.1 The Value of Social Connections at Work

Social activities are frequently seen as optional in many workplaces, and they may be the first to be discontinued during periods of cost-cutting or heightened performance focus. However, it is a mistake that can have far-reaching detrimental effects to downplay the significance of social relationships in the workplace. Good relationships with others are not merely a "nice-to-have"; they are essential to any team's success and operation.

- **Improving Cooperation:** Effective collaboration requires trust and camaraderie, both of which are fostered by social ties. Employees are more inclined to support one another, speak honestly, and exchange ideas when they know one another outside of work. Because of this trust, people are more inclined to seek assistance, offer helpful criticism, or take the chance of coming up with novel solutions when working on projects.

- **Enhancing Workplace Contentment:** Workers who experience a sense of belonging and job satisfaction are more likely to be socially connected at work. These connections foster a positive work atmosphere where staff members are more driven and dedicated to their jobs. A workplace that inhibits social connection, on the other hand, might make employees feel isolated, which can result in disengagement and even higher turnover rates.

- **Developing Emotional Hardiness:** One important component of stress management at work is social support. Employees are better able to cope with the demands of their jobs when they have strong social ties. These relationships give people a feeling of community, emotional outlets, and ways to unwind, all of which support resilience in trying circumstances. Employees are deprived of an essential tool for preserving their mental and emotional health when their workplace discourages or undervalues these relationships.

One of the cultural strengths is How well a company's employees get along is typically a reflection of its culture. Social ties strengthen common beliefs and standards, fostering a harmonious and upbeat culture that becomes ingrained in the organization's identity. Without these ties, culture may break apart, resulting in miscommunication, a lack of team cohesion, and misunderstandings.

Organizations risk failure if they fail to recognize the value of social ties. Establishing solid bonds between coworkers is essential to a robust, cooperative, and healthy team. Businesses may make sure that their teams work more efficiently, stay engaged, and are better prepared to overcome obstacles as a team by fostering these relationships.

7.2 Promoting Social Engagement to Increase Productivity

Many people think that letting workers interact will make

them less productive. Some businesses adopt a rigid stance, prohibiting extracurricular activities and restricting casual contacts. Nonetheless, studies continually demonstrate that social engagement actually increases productivity rather than decreasing it.

1. **Breaks Improve Mental Acuity:** Employees can take a break from their work, clear their heads, and return to work with fresh focus when they take regular breaks that incorporate social engagement. Cognitive weariness can be lessened by brief social breaks, which improves decision-making and produces higher-quality work.

1. **Promoting Cooperation and Teamwork:** Informal discussions frequently result in fruitful partnerships. Workers from various teams or departments can exchange ideas and insights that wouldn't be discussed in official meetings. Cross-functional synergies are produced by these natural interactions, where the total is larger than the sum of its parts. Businesses enable creative ideas to emerge by promoting informal discussions, which improves

problem-solving and boosts output.

1. **Enhancing Worker Involvement:** Employee engagement is directly impacted by social interactions at work as well. Employees are more involved in their work and have a greater stake in the company's success when they feel socially linked to their peers. In addition to being more productive, engaged workers are also more inclined to go above and beyond the call of duty to support company objectives, mentor coworkers, or volunteer for projects.

- **Decreased Absenteeism and Burnout:** Burnout and absenteeism are also decreased by promoting social connections. Workers are more likely to communicate when they are feeling overburdened and ask for help before they become exhausted if they perceive that their coworkers are supporting them. A more balanced, healthful workplace is produced by this sense of community, where people are empowered to handle stress in more constructive ways.

Progressive businesses understand that socializing is an essential part of a productive workplace and do not see it as a distraction. Businesses may create an atmosphere where workers feel engaged, inspired, and better equipped to produce their best work by providing areas and chances for casual contacts.

7.3 Establishing a Connective Culture

Encouraging social interaction among coworkers is more than just letting them chat during breaks. It entails proactively fostering a culture that values camaraderie, community, and support amongst individuals. It takes deliberate leadership work and organized chances for staff members to interact with one another to create this kind of culture.

- **Events for Team Building:** Organizing team-building activities is one of the best strategies to strengthen social ties. These can include informal in-office events like luncheons or happy hours as well as off-site retreats and training. The secret is to establish a space where workers may socialize in a laid-back, non-work context, enabling them to know one another as people rather than just colleagues. Additionally, by strengthening ties across departments, these gatherings can aid in dismantling organizational silos and promoting cooperation.

- **Interest groups and employee clubs:** Another strategy to promote social relationships is to encourage staff members to start clubs or interest groups based on common interests or passions. These organizations may concentrate on volunteer work, book clubs, wellness, or fitness. Employees who participate in these groups feel more a part of the larger company community, which improves their sense of belonging in addition to strengthening interpersonal ties.

- **Establishing Unofficial Areas:** Social contact can also be promoted via physical workspaces. Businesses can plan their workspaces to include unofficial spaces like coffee shops or lounges where staff members are welcome to stop by and chat.

These areas contribute to the development of an accessible and open culture where unplanned encounters are not just accepted but actively promoted.

- A list of mentorship programs Building relationships between staff members at various organizational levels can be facilitated by a well-designed mentorship program. In addition to promoting knowledge exchange, matching junior staff members or new hires with more seasoned mentors fosters a supportive bond that can increase a person's sense of belonging to the company. These connections can go beyond career advancement and strengthen the connection culture as a whole.

- Opportunities for Inclusive Socialization: Leadership must make sure that social events are welcoming and serve a diverse staff. Providing a range of options is essential to making sure that everyone feels welcome, as certain employees may not feel comfortable attending particular kinds of social activities. While some workers may do better in larger, more dynamic environments, others may prefer smaller, more intimate meetings. Every employee should be given the chance to participate in ways that suit their comfort levels and individual preferences should be respected in a culture of connectedness.

Planning events is only one aspect of fostering a culture of connection; another is integrating social interaction into the very fabric of the company. Employees are more inclined to help one another, collaborate well, and contribute to a supportive, cooperative work environment when they feel connected to one another. Connection-focused businesses benefit from increased employee satisfaction, improved teamwork, and eventually improved company results.

Social interaction at work is not a diversion; rather, it is essential to the success of the company. Strong social ties promote teamwork, increase output, and establish a feeling of community, all of which increase job satisfaction and employee retention. Businesses that restrict social connection run the danger of developing a disengaged and isolated staff, which can lead to a decline in creativity, poor communication, and low morale.

Social connection doesn't have to be expensive or time-consuming to promote. Company culture can be significantly impacted by small actions like employee clubs, team-building activities, or setting up casual gathering places. Businesses can strengthen their teams, lower employee burnout, and achieve long-term success by aggressively fostering a culture of connection. Social interaction is crucial to creating a successful, resilient, and effective organization; it is not a diversion from work.

CHAPTER 8

Using Pizza to Fill in the Gaps

8.1 Cultural Issues Are Not Solved by Surface-Level Solutions

Leadership frequently resorts to short-term solutions, such as providing free pizza, refreshments, or branded items, to raise spirits when employee dissatisfaction or low morale is prevalent in many firms. Although these actions may temporarily foster goodwill, they are essentially band-aid fixes that fail to address the root causes of a company's culture problems. Employees eventually come to view these initiatives as brief diversion from more pressing issues.

- **The Myth of Boosting Morale:** Although it's a fleeting illusion, free food, events, or minor benefits might produce an instant impression of happiness. These short-term boosts just cover up the symptoms without addressing the underlying causes, such as inadequate leadership, poor communication, or a lack of opportunity for professional advancement. In actuality, depending too much on these band-aid solutions might backfire, making workers feel condescending or underappreciated while the underlying problems still exist.

- **Workers Recognize Token Motions:** Authenticity in the workplace is valued by today's workforce, especially the younger generations. Workers are more likely to notice when management is using benefits as a cover for important changes. Employees start to distrust leadership when they believe that these benefits are a diversion from more pressing problems like unfair treatment, toxic management, or an unclear corporate mission. In a time when employee opinion is frequently shared on sites like Glassdoor and LinkedIn, this mistrust can result in increased disengagement, more turnover, and a bad reputation for the business.

- **Inaccurate Remedies for Pervasive Problems:**

Deeper issues like a lack of transparency, unfair labor practices, or an unclear business vision won't be resolved by a pizza party or a new branded water bottle. Management frequently views these short cuts as a means of avoiding more difficult problems that call for genuine effort, such as reorganizing leadership, enhancing lines of communication, or resolving workload disparities. Employers who use such flimsy tactics run the danger of alienating staff members, who will believe that their genuine issues are not being taken seriously.

Businesses that use material benefits and incentives to patch up cultural rifts are ignoring the structural problems that ultimately determine employee engagement and satisfaction. Deep cultural change, not fleeting distractions, is the source of true change.

8.2 Sincere Attempts to Enhance Culture

Addressing the underlying reasons of employee discontent necessitates a purposeful and sincere attempt to improve business culture. Cultural change necessitates a continuous dedication to comprehending and enhancing the work experience; it cannot be accomplished with one-time projects or superficial benefits.

- **Resolving the Fundamental Reasons for Discontent:** Organizations must investigate the root reasons of dissatisfaction rather than focusing only on the symptoms. Common problems include toxic management practices, unclear responsibilities and expectations, poor leadership communication, and insufficient recognition. Leadership must be prepared to take on these issues head-on and develop solutions in order to boost engagement and morale. This could entail reorganizing teams, reviewing pay plans, putting leadership development initiatives into place, or communicating the company's objectives and vision more openly.

- **Dedication to Honest Communication:** Transparency is essential to a thriving culture. Employers need to aggressively solicit employee input and create a culture where employees may voice issues without fear of reprisal. Frequent town halls, one-on-one meetings, and anonymous feedback platforms are useful methods for determining the mood of the workforce. Leadership should be receptive to criticism and show that they genuinely want to hear what others have to say and take appropriate action. When workers perceive that their opinions are respected and heard, they are more inclined to become involved and dedicated.

- **Building a Feeling of Meaning and Community:** Developing a feeling of purpose among staff members is another important aspect of enhancing culture. Employees want to feel that they are a part of something greater than themselves and that their contributions are valued. Companies should make sure that all levels of employees understand how their job contributes to the organization's objectives and effectively communicate their mission, vision, and values. In addition to raising spirits, a feeling of unity also encourages devotion and drive.

- **The Function of Leadership in Cultural Transformation:** The top is where change begins.

Leaders must set an example by living up to the ideals they want to inculcate in the culture. If leadership does not exhibit these qualities themselves, a culture of respect, cooperation, and creativity cannot thrive. Executives and managers must hold themselves accountable for the changes they want to make and be outspoken advocates for the intended culture change.

A consistent, calculated strategy that tackles the underlying reasons of discontent and establishes a basis of openness, trust, and a common goal is necessary for cultural change. Businesses can only foster an environment where workers feel appreciated, involved, and inspired by committing to this deeper work.

8.3 Appreciation of Employees Beyond Tangible Benefits

Benefits like free lunches or branded items are nice, but they should never be used as a replacement for sincere appreciation of workers' efforts and achievements. When done properly, recognition has a big impact on raising engagement, improving morale, and creating a healthy workplace culture.

- **The Influence of Genuine Appreciation**: Workers want to believe that their leadership and peers value and acknowledge their work. Genuine acknowledgment recognizes the unique contributions that each member of the team makes to the team's success, going beyond public acclaim or awards. This kind of acknowledgment should be prompt, genuine, and closely related to the worker's accomplishments to demonstrate that their special efforts are appreciated.

- **Customized Recognition Techniques:** Not every employee reacts to the same kind of acknowledgment. While some may value private, one-on-one comments, others would prefer public recognition. Team members' preferences should be understood by leadership so that awards can be tailored to their needs. While professional development opportunities or the opportunity to take on additional tasks may be the finest forms of acknowledgment for some employees, words of affirmation may have the most impact for others.

- **In addition to material rewards:** Bonuses and gift cards are examples of material benefits, but they are not a substitute for a culture of appreciation. Through both official and informal avenues, recognition should be included into daily operations. Peer-to-peer recognition programs, leadership shout-outs, and customized thank-you notes are a few examples of this. A positive feedback loop is created when employees receive consistent acknowledgment for their hard work, which motivates them to keep up their excellent work.

- **Engagement and Retention Are Driven by Recognition:** One of the main factors influencing employee engagement and retention is recognition. Employees are more likely to stick with their company, be more productive, and take on more responsibility if they feel valued. Conversely, a lack of acknowledgment can result in resentment, apathy, and eventually increased turnover. Giving employees material incentives is insufficient; they also need to believe that their work is valued and plays a significant role in the company's success.

Businesses can foster an atmosphere where workers feel appreciated beyond the monetary benefits they receive by emphasizing sincere, customized acknowledgment. Acknowledgment creates a culture of gratitude, improves team dynamics, and inspires workers to keep doing excellent work.

In many workplaces, there is a widespread but incorrect desire to address underlying culture issues with surface-level solutions like free food or company merchandise. These benefits could temporarily raise spirits, but they don't address the underlying issues that lead to employee discontent or disengagement. When leaders make these gestures to delay making substantive changes, employees rapidly pick it up, which can cause trust to break down and frustration to rise.

Real, sustained attempts to address root causes like inadequate communication, a lack of acknowledgment, or toxic management techniques are necessary for true culture change. Businesses may foster a culture where workers feel appreciated and inspired by making investments in open communication, genuine acknowledgment, and a feeling of purpose. In particular, recognition must be genuine and go beyond financial benefits to show gratitude for each person's contributions.

In the end, companies that approach cultural transformation strategically and thoughtfully will cultivate a more engaged, healthy workforce that is better able to propel long-term success. Pizza cannot be used to cover up real cultural change; instead, a dedication to tackling the underlying issues that affect worker satisfaction and organizational effectiveness is needed.

CHAPTER 9

Cultural Imposition vs. Cultural Development

9.1 Culture is Not Forced; It Is Organic

Any organization's culture encompasses much more than just its mission, laws, and procedures. It is an ever-changing and dynamic force that develops naturally from the contacts, activities, and common ideals of the individuals that make up the organization. A workplace that feels forced or unauthentic is frequently the result of leadership's attempts to impose culture through strict directives.

- **The Character of Organic Culture:** Over time, a positive corporate culture emerges organically as staff members meaningfully interact with leadership and one another. Mutual respect, shared beliefs, and shared experiences form the foundation of this kind of culture. Because it represents the actual attitudes and behaviors of the individuals in the organization rather than a set of fabricated expectations, culture that develops organically is more robust.

- **The Drawbacks of Cultural Imposition:** Leadership runs the danger of causing a rift between management and staff when it tries to enforce a preset culture from the top down. Workers who believe their opinions and values are not represented in the cultural narrative being promoted may view these initiatives as inauthentic. Because they feel under pressure to fit in with standards that don't match their own experiences or values, forced cultures can cause disengagement among employees.

- **Promoting Organic Development:** Leadership can influence the culture, but it's crucial to understand that culture cannot be controlled. Leadership should instead concentrate on establishing the ideal environment for culture to develop naturally. This entails giving staff members the appropriate resources, setting, and latitude to add to the company's culture. In this process, it is essential to listen to employees, value their opinions, and promote open communication.

To put it briefly, culture is something that develops organically within a company and is influenced by both the workforce as a whole and the leadership. Businesses can avoid the problems of a forced, top-down approach and instead create a more genuine and long-lasting work environment by acknowledging that culture is organic.

9.2 The Function of Leadership in Fostering Culture

Although everyone in the business ultimately shapes its culture, leadership is essential to fostering and directing its growth. Leadership ideals and actions are the cornerstones upon which a robust and wholesome culture can be established. Leadership must, however, view culture as a continuous, cooperative process rather than a set of rules if it is to flourish.

- **Establishing the Scene:** Setting the initial tone for the company's culture is the responsibility of the leadership. Living and demonstrating the principles that the business upholds is more important than enforcing a strict set of regulations. Leaders that behave honorably, openly, and with respect provide a strong model for the rest of the company to follow. When leaders live up to the principles they want to see in the workplace, it communicates to staff that these ideals are a living reality rather than just words on paper.

- **Establishing the Conditions for Development:** The culture can be sown by the leadership, but it also needs the proper conditions to flourish. This entails creating an environment at work where workers are free to express themselves, exchange ideas, and help shape the culture. Leaders should actively solicit employee input, maintain open channels of communication, and be flexible as the culture changes. When workers believe their contributions to the culture are appreciated and acknowledged, they are working in a nurturing setting.

- **The promotion of ownership:** A strong culture is one where workers take pride in their work. Because of this, leaders must act more as facilitators than as enforcers. Leaders should encourage staff members to actively shape culture rather than prescribing how it should evolve. Leadership establishes a more genuine and long-lasting culture by giving teams the freedom to determine the company's values and how they are embodied in daily operations.

It is the responsibility of leadership to foster culture rather than impose it. Leaders may direct the creation of a culture that is resilient and authentic by fostering an atmosphere of openness and cooperation, promoting employee ownership, and setting a good example.

9.3 Fostering a Culture of Collaboration

Employees at all levels must work together to create a corporate culture; leadership is not the only person responsible for this. A cooperative approach to culture-building guarantees that the values, experiences, and goals of the entire organization—not just those at the top—are reflected in the company's culture. As a result, the workplace becomes more genuine, inclusive, and engaged.

- **Employee Involvement in Culture Development:** Workers provide a variety of viewpoints, experiences, and concepts. Leadership can guarantee that the company's values accurately represent the workforce by incorporating them in the culture development process. Regular feedback sessions, employee surveys, and seminars that ask staff members to express their ideas on the culture they would want to see in the company can all help achieve this. Employees are more likely to accept responsibility for the culture and actively contribute to its success when they feel included in the process.

- **Building on Values in Common:** A culture that is based on shared principles rather than imposed ideals is said to be collaborative. Employees and leadership should collaborate to determine which core values are most ingrained in the company before creating plans to incorporate those values into routine operations. This could entail outlining the practical manifestations of principles like honesty, creativity, or cooperation as well as how they can be strengthened by corporate regulations, incentives, and recognition initiatives.

- **Encouraging Collaboration and Team-Building:** Building a great culture requires promoting teamwork. This can be accomplished through casual social encounters, cross-departmental projects, and team-building exercises that foster relationships and improve collaboration among staff members. Leadership builds a culture of cooperation and mutual support by facilitating opportunities for collaboration, which fortifies the company's overall cultural fabric.

- **Constant Participation and Adjustment:** Culture building is a continuous process that calls for constant participation and adjustment. The company's culture must change and grow with it. Leadership should use performance measures, employee input, and general job satisfaction to evaluate the culture on a regular basis. To keep the culture in line with the objectives and core values of the business, changes should be made when needed.

Employees at all levels must contribute to the team effort that is developing a collaborative culture. Leadership may establish a culture that is genuine, inclusive, and flexible enough to meet the evolving demands of the company by establishing a foundation of shared values, encouraging teamwork, and consistently interacting with the workforce.

There is a significant distinction between enforcing a culture and creating one. Top-down instructions or one-size-fits-all policies cannot impose culture; rather, it must develop naturally with involvement from all members of the organization. Although leadership is essential in fostering and directing this process, they must acknowledge that the workforce's collective behaviors, values, and experiences ultimately form culture.

A good culture is one that emerges organically over time, with employees helping to build it and leaders establishing the tone. Businesses may create a culture that is robust and true to the organization's essence by emphasizing cooperation, inclusivity, and ongoing engagement.

Building a culture fosters a sense of ownership, belonging, and shared purpose, whereas imposing one results in disengagement and disconnection. Leadership needs to concentrate on establishing the ideal conditions for culture to thrive, encouraging teamwork, and making sure the culture is long-lasting and genuine.

CHAPTER 10

FOR THE SAKE OF SURVEYS

10.1 Survey Fatigue: An Issue

Surveys are now frequently used in today's business environment to assess employee satisfaction, comprehend workplace culture, and pinpoint areas in need of development. However, "survey fatigue," a condition where employees lose interest in the feedback process because they are asked for their comments too frequently, might result from the frequent administration of surveys. The general workplace culture and the efficacy of surveys may both be seriously harmed by this weariness.

The absence of actionability Employees start to view surveys as merely formalities rather than sincere attempts to promote participation when they observe that their feedback routinely does not lead to noticeable changes or improvements. Employees may feel that their opinions are unimportant as a result of this attitude, which can lead to a sense of hopelessness and less deliberate responses.

- **The Fatal Cycle:** Feedback quality declines as engagement declines. In a feedback cycle that perpetuates the very problems the surveys were designed to address, employees may give hurried answers out of disinterest or aggravation. Employees may feel their opinions are ignored in a toxic company culture if survey results are not meaningfully addressed.

- **The decline of trust:** Employee faith in leadership might also be damaged by survey weariness. Employees may doubt the sincerity and reasons behind surveys that are carried out without a clear goal or follow-up. A culture of cynicism rather than cooperation may result from this mistrust, harming the relationship between management and employees.

Organizations must put survey quality above quantity in order to fight survey weariness. Companies should concentrate on meaningful, well-structured surveys that are linked to certain objectives rather than conducting surveys on a regular basis. This strategy aids in making sure that worker input is respected and that the procedure itself stays interesting and pertinent.

10.2 Using Input to Take Action

Surveying employees to get their opinions is just the beginning of creating a positive work environment. How businesses use the information obtained from surveys is what really makes them valuable. Maintaining employee trust and exhibiting a sincere commitment to improvement require acting on feedback.

- **Explaining the Objective:** Leadership must explain the goal of the surveys and the intended use of the input after the findings have been gathered. Openness regarding the decision-making process promotes trust and enables staff members to realize how valued and significant their contributions are.

- **Creating Plans of Action:** Following the collection

and analysis of input, leadership should develop workable plans that tackle the main issues raised by the surveys. This could entail particular programs designed to solve workload concerns, boost communication, or improve staff well-being. Leadership shows that they are dedicated to resolving employee complaints and creating a positive work environment by providing clear guidelines.

- **Involving Workers in Solutions:** Employee collaboration and buy-in can be improved by involving them in the creation of action plans. Leadership may foster a sense of empowerment and ownership among staff members by asking them to offer suggestions for enhancements. In addition to fostering the development of creative solutions, this cooperative method serves to reaffirm that employee opinions are respected.

- **Responsibility and Monitoring:** Leadership must hold themselves responsible for carrying out the changes after action plans have been created. Giving staff regular updates on developments, difficulties, and future measures shows that management is dedicated to fostering a flexible and responsive work environment. Employee engagement and trust are increased by this transparency.

Organizations can show their dedication to ongoing development and foster a work environment that values employee input by successfully implementing feedback. This strategy encourages a more engaged and motivated staff in addition to reducing survey fatigue.

10.3 Assessing Development After the Survey

Following the implementation of modifications based on survey responses, businesses need to set up a system for tracking their performance and growth. Employee contributions are acknowledged and the value of their input in promoting constructive change is reaffirmed when progress is tracked and communicated.

- **Setting Up Metrics:** To evaluate the success of modifications made in response to survey responses, organizations should create certain measures. These measures could be productivity levels, retention rates, employee satisfaction ratings, or qualitative input from follow-up surveys. Organizations can assess the results of their projects and pinpoint areas for improvement by establishing clear standards.

- **Transparency in Results Sharing:** To make sure that workers feel appreciated and included in the process, communication is essential. Updates on survey initiative progress should be shared on a regular basis by organizations, emphasizing both areas of success and those that still face difficulties. Employees feel more accountable as a result of this transparency, which also demonstrates to them that their opinions matter.

- **Asking for Continuous Input:** Measuring shouldn't be done just once. Establishing systems for continual feedback can help organizations evaluate the success of their improvements over time. This could entail informal check-ins with staff members, focus groups, or follow-up questionnaires. Organizations can show their dedication to ongoing development and make necessary adjustments to their strategy by keeping lines of communication open.

- **Honoring Accomplishments:** Employee engagement and morale can be greatly raised by acknowledging and appreciating accomplishments brought about by employee input. In addition to reaffirming the importance of employees' contributions, praising them fosters a culture of gratitude and acknowledgment.

In the end, tracking results after a survey is crucial to confirming the value of employee input and making sure businesses are attentive to their requirements. Organizations can foster a culture that values feedback and promotes continuous improvement by setting clear metrics, speaking openly, asking for frequent feedback, and acknowledging accomplishments.

Surveys are effective instruments for determining employee mood and promoting constructive change inside a company. They can, however, result in survey weariness, disengagement, and a breakdown of confidence between staff and management if they are carried out carelessly or without follow-up. Organizations must prioritize relevant feedback, transform insights into change that can be implemented, and regularly assess and share progress if they want to fully utilize surveys.

Organizations may establish a dynamic workplace culture that rewards involvement, encourages continual development, and ultimately propels success by tackling the issues of survey fatigue, cultivating an accountability culture, and acknowledging employee accomplishments. By adopting this strategy, surveys are transformed from a mundane activity into a potent tool for organizational development and cultural change.

ABOUT THE AUTHOR

 Renowned business strategist, author, and consultant James Royce Smartman has over twenty years of experience in a variety of fields, including corporate management, entrepreneurship, and finance. James has a strong academic background and an MBA from a prestigious university. As a result, he has a good understanding of the nuances of contemporary business practices and market dynamics.

James has held executive positions in multiple Fortune 500 businesses over his career, effectively leading projects that have sparked efficiency, growth, and innovation. Because of his special combination of theoretical knowledge and real-world experience, he can offer organizations of all sizes frameworks and concrete tactics.

James is regularly asked to speak at conferences and seminars as a thought leader in the business sector, offering his knowledge on subjects including strategic planning, organizational behavior, and leadership development. In addition, he frequently contributes his thoughts on new trends and best practices to eminent business journals.

James Royce Smartman is devoted to helping company executives and entrepreneurs realize their objectives by providing them with creative solutions and useful guidance. His writings seek to demystify difficult business ideas so that readers of all skill levels can understand and use them. James offers a road map for success that is in line with the changing business environment of today by emphasizing practical examples and tried-and-true tactics.

James regularly mentors young professionals and supports different business projects that foster entrepreneurship and innovation in addition to his writing and consulting work. He promotes an organizational culture that welcomes change and encourages expansion because he believes in the value of teamwork and ongoing education.

www.ingramcontent.com/pod-product-compliance
Lightning Source LLC
Chambersburg PA
CBHW050319230526
45471CB00005B/2262